MW00762586

MIDDLE AGE CAREER CHANGE

HOW TO TURN YOUR LIFE PASSION INTO A CAREER

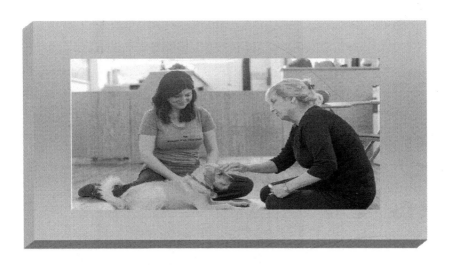

Middle age career change

By Beverly Hill

Introduction

I want to thank you and congratulate you for choosing the book, *"**MIDDLE AGE CAREER CHANGE: How to Turn Your Life Passion into a Career**"*.

You're reading this book because you currently find yourself in a middle age career change, or you're looking for information to help someone you know who is in this situation, right? In the current job market we find ourselves in, career changes are really not all that surprising. So being prepared for how to respond to them is clearly a logical step to take.

Unemployment numbers are absolutely through the roof, and this is one involuntary reason you may be looking to make a career switch. On the flip side of the coin, when companies downsize their workforce, the remaining employees are left behind to try and accomplish a 5 person job with a 2 person team, and no increase in pay. This can lead to job dissatisfaction, and could be a reason you're looking into making a midlife career change today. Of course, there are some people who would be frustrated with their choice of career in ANY market economy, and a career change for them would be inevitable.

Many people who find themselves caught in the middle of a midlife career change panic immediately. For most people, their job is what defines them as a person. When someone asks you to tell a little about yourself, it usually ends up sounding a lot like a job description. As a society, that's how we've been conditioned. This terror, though, can lead to some severe lapses in judgment.

The person may jump on the first opportunity that presents itself, without really taking any time to evaluate whether that position will be a good move for them or not. This is a horrible way to make any decision, and especially one that can have as critical an impact on a person's life as a career move. So, what factors should a person consider in making a middle age career change? Join me in CHAPTER ONE as I proceed to discuss, how to reinvent yourself.

Thanks again for choosing this book, I hope you enjoy it!

ABOUT THE AUTHOR

Beverly Hill is a sociologist. She is the CEO of C.E.F Associates and formerly served as head of department of sociology in Premier Natural Resources Inc.

A graduate of Nelson High School also graduated from the University of Toronto with a B.A in economics and finance and holds an M.S from Cambridge University in public relations and PhD in sociology.

She has written many articles on human equality, environmental issues, personal development and peace keeping in different newspapers. She has also appeared in many magazines and is frequently interviewed for articles on family, race, socioeconomic status, and how to survive in your environment. She has also worked on the importance of health of relationship between parents and children. Her book 'The Middle Child' focuses on the importance of the attention given to the children and what to expect from them. This book helps parents understand their children.

In addition to these works she is also the author of 'Surviving Alone ' which is about her own childhood growing up; she writes about her family struggles living on a low income budget and growing her own food to survive.

C.E.F Associates formed in 1999 in Idaho, USA she worked both nationally and internationally. This is a consulting company which has clients all over the world. Ms. Hill the CEO of the company is the main reason of the huge client base because of her servings in foreign countries.

TABLE OF CONTENT

© **Copyright 2017 by Holistic Measures, LLC - All rights reserved.**

This document is geared towards providing exact and reliable information in regards to the topic and issue covered. The publication is sold with the idea that the publisher is not required to render accounting, officially permitted, or otherwise, qualified services. If advice is necessary, legal or professional, a practiced individual in the profession should be ordered.

- From a Declaration of Principles which was accepted and approved equally by a Committee of the American Bar Association and a Committee of Publishers and Associations.

In no way is it legal to reproduce, duplicate, or transmit any part of this document in either electronic means or in printed format. Recording of this publication is strictly prohibited and any storage of this document is not allowed unless with written permission from the publisher. All rights reserved.

The information provided herein is stated to be truthful and consistent, in that any liability, in terms of inattention or otherwise, by any usage or abuse of any policies, processes, or directions contained within is the solitary and utter responsibility of the recipient reader. Under no circumstances will any legal responsibility or blame be held against the publisher for any reparation, damages, or monetary loss due to the information herein, either directly or indirectly.

Respective authors own all copyrights not held by the publisher.

The information herein is offered for informational purposes solely, and is universal as so. The presentation of the information is without contract or any type of guarantee assurance.

The trademarks that are used are without any consent, and the publication of the trademark is without permission or backing by the trademark owner. All trademarks and brands within this book are for clarifying purposes only and are the owned by the owners themselves, not affiliated with this document.

Chapter 1

MIDDLE AGE CAREER CHANGE

Living in a world with the financial system limping along with a high percent unemployment rate, it's not unusual for even the gainfully employed to test free agency, and see what else might be available. In a 2009 Salary.com survey, when global financial markets were still plummeting, more than 65 percent of workers said they were actively looking for new jobs.

It's one thing to change jobs, something most people will do more than 10 times between the ages of 18 and 42, but it's quite another to change careers. Making the leap from a field in which you've been trained and have experience to a new one takes careful consideration planning, and the right expectations.

This is true of anyone interested in making a change, but what about professionals who have been in the workforce for 20 or 30-plus years? Baby boomers, born between 1946 and 1964, make up 40 percent of the labor force, and shifting gears later in life to focus on new career objectives can be challenging, but also rewarding. Seasoned professionals often have a different perspective than their younger colleagues. Middle-aged workers usually place more value on nonmonetary benefits, such as less stress, flexible work schedules, and personal fulfillment, so when they're able to change careers they can make the jump to areas that are more professionally fulfilling rather than having to worry about how much they earn.

Chapter 2

HOW TO PLAN AHEAD FOR A MID-LIFE CAREER CHANGE

Sitting in your cubicle daydreaming about becoming the manager of the Boston Red Sox may seem like a good way to plan for your next career, but it's unlikely to get you anywhere. If you're seriously considering making the leap, it's going to take planning and lots of it. As we mentioned earlier, the national unemployment rate in the United States is high; as of June 2011, it was hovering at more than 9 percent. That means the competition for existing jobs is fierce. For a little perspective, consider that for every job that opens, there are five people unemployed. That statistic has increased from 1.7 unemployed people for every opening during the three years before the 2008 economic collapse. Nothing in the world intimidating about that, is there?

The first thing most employees do when they consider making a professional change is evaluate their current situation. Is the work fulfilling? Does it make good use of their skills? Notice that all potential reasons for a job change, but not necessarily a career overhaul. So be honest with yourself about the actual work you're doing, and try to be as objective as possible. Bosses come and go, so if your job is fulfilling except for a few variables, work on changing those before looking to make the leap into a new career. For middle-age workers, chances are good that you are the boss; therefore, you may have more control over your situation than more junior-level professionals.

The next step is to evaluate this potential career shift to see how it matches up with your needs. You're leaving a career in which you have a certain level of seniority, and presumably, earn more than someone just entering that field. Take a long, hard look at whether you want to put in the longer hours and shorter pay that sometimes come with being the new kid on the block. Neither of these factors should keep you from going for it, just plan on setting aside a financial cushion, or altering your lifestyle if you know a career change will result in pay decrease. Do this by getting militant about "needs" vs. "wants", and trimming the fat from your day-to-day budget. Consider these sacrifices and investment in the new career.

Once you've decided that you want to move forward with a change, the next step will be to make sure you're prepared to actually do the job.

Chapter 3

HOW TO SET YOURSELF UP FOR A SUCCESSFUL MID-LIFE CAREER CHANGE

Ok, so you've decided to take the plunge and make a career change. Not only that, but you also have a pretty good idea what you want to do, and how making this transition is going to affect your lifestyle. Good work. Now it's time to make sure you're actually qualified to enter your chosen second career.

But first, make sure you can get in the door.

The so-called "gray ceiling" puts middle-age workers at a disadvantage, because younger professionals will work for less pay, are easier to manage, and will cost the company less because they tend to have fewer medical issues. Education, particularly in today's automated digital workplaces, can be a significant obstacle for older workers. Older workers are seen as been less tech-savvy, and in today's highly automated, ultra digital work environment, this is a big disadvantage.

So the trick is to demonstrate that your skills have kept pace with changes. Even if the work you're interested in doing doesn't change over time, you still want to show that you're up on the latest trends. This can easily be reflected in an updated resume that demonstrates proficiency in emerging technology and business trends, including social networking, and personal computing, in addition to job-specific skills.

To further bolster the potential for middle-aged workers, many colleges and universities offer degree programs designed specifically for this group. Entry into these programs usually depends on experience and acumen rather than academic or test performance. Once a perspective boss knows you handle the job, the scales tip considerably in favor of people with years of experience. Mature workers are viewed as loyal, honest and punctual, among a host of other attributes.

Now that you've landed that dream gig, it's time to make sure you hit the ground running.

Chapter 4

FINDING SUCCESS IN YOUR SECOND CAREER

We discussed the differing perspectives of those brand-new to the workforce, and those who've been around the block. Once the second career has been embarked upon, the older worker once again has the advantage.

In a 2009 AARP study, 91 percent of workers who were 51 or older when they changed jobs said they were happier as a result. Less stress, more flexibility were the reasons cited, which, you'll remember from the introduction, are both leading reasons for seeking a change in the first place.

And because mid-life workers are often more focused on personal fulfillment, rather than climbing the corporate ladder, they can concentrate on the work instead of angling for the boss's favor. This translates into added value for the employer. According to a study released by Bank of America Corp., 94 percent of employers think it's important to retain older workers. To do this, companies are offering scheduling options, telecommuting policies, and retirement planning, and the statistics are bearing out the value companies are placing on senior staff. In May 2011, the U.S. unemployment rate for workers 55 and over was 6.8 percent, several points lower than the national average.

Finally, this is the area that may be causing the most hand-wringing, be prepared to report to someone younger than you—maybe a lot younger. Bridging this potential generational gap will be a big factor in how much fulfillment you get from your new role.

There are a few ways to do this. First, avoid making generalizations. Not everyone born after 1980 is a slacker, honest. Plus, if you can demonstrate early a few key competencies (particularly in the areas of technology or new media), you can help obliterate any prejudices they may have toward the older crowd. Another way to make this relationship work is by encouraging feedback. One of the stereotypes that dogs older workers is that they're set in their ways. Crush this right off the bat by actively soliciting input from younger team members. Finally, don't be afraid to exert your experience. If you have something to offer, don't keep it to yourself! Making a career change is never easy, and doing so later in life carries its own set of challenges. But as you can see, with a little preparation, it's much more manageable than you might think.

Chapter 5

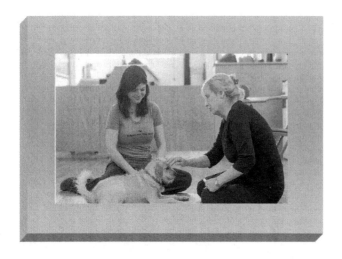

Middle age career change

HOW TO TURN YOUR LIFE PASSION INTO A CAREER

Imagine your very favorite activity. Maybe you love to knit or sew. Maybe you're obsessed with movies or theater. Now, imagine quitting your day job, and getting paid to work at the thing you love the most. Many fantasize about turning their pastimes into full-time gigs, but actually making the leap is a little bit tougher. It takes research, planning, and plain old hard work.

Unless you're independently wealthy, you can't just quit your job to pursue a new career without preparing. You need to be able to keep paying your bill as you pursue your passion, and you need to make sure you have the skills necessary to succeed at this new endeavor. Whether your vision involves self-employment, or working for your dream company, you probably can't just shift careers overnight.

Whether you're looking for a career change, or aiming to transition your hobby into a full-time job, it can seem like a pretty daunting task. With some planning, and a few tricks, you just might be able to get paid to do what you love.

Chapter 6

7 TIPS ON HOW TO CHANGE WHAT YOU LOVE INTO A CAREER
Be Realistic

Talk to some people who are doing the job you're after. There's often a big difference between the career you fantasize about, and the day-to-day reality of turning a hobby into a full-time gig. If you love antiquing, you might dream of opening an antique shop of your own. Remember, though, it's not all about scouting out great finds. You have to deal with taxes, accounting, and business licenses. For many people, it's worth sorting through the more mundane details in order to do what you love, but make sure you don't take the plunge with stars in your eyes.

This is another case where the informational interview can be a big help. Ask about the day-to-day responsibilities of the job you want, and what it's like to work at that particular company. Few jobs are as fun in practice as they seem to an outsider, and getting a clear picture of your potential new work environment can help you ensure that you don't end up disappointed.

Think Outside the Box

Maybe you don't have the skill set for your dream career, but that doesn't mean you have to give up. Look for other jobs within the same industry that will make you just as happy. For example, if you love movies, but don't have the technical skills to be a director, check out what positions are available that would let you be close to the action, and use the skills that you already have. It's also a good idea to consider what you really want out of a dream career. Maybe it's not so much the job itself that's your passion, but what the job allows you to do. If you love to travel, for example, you might want to look at working for an airline, or a tour company.

If you want to work for yourself, you might need to find creative ways to make ends meet while you get your business off the ground. Can you take a part-time job that isn't too taxing, or take on some freelance work in the evenings that leaves your days free to focus on the business that you're really passionate about? Diversifying you income streams helps keep you more financially stable during tough economic times.

Work on Your Resume and Cover Letter

Your current resume and cover letter may have been perfect for impressing your current employer, but if you're looking for a career change, you need to spruce them up to match your ambitions. If you're working in the tech field now, and want to move into something more creative, for example, you'll want to change up your resume to focus on your creative skills. This is called creating a "targeted resume." Do some research to see what key skills your ideal employers are looking for, and feature them prominently in your resume.

The same goes for your cover letter. You want to sum up your skills and explain, point by point, why you're the most qualified candidate for the position. If someone from within the company referred you, the cover letter is a good place to mention it. Many companies give extra weight to applicants who have an internal referral.

Network, Network, Network

It might sound trite, but in many industries, it really is all about who you know. It's a lot easier to get an interview if someone within the company vouches for you, so get out there, and meet people in your desired field. Scope out some local business networking events, grab your business cards, and start schmoozing. You can also set up an informational interview, where you chat with someone in the industry to get a feel for what you need to know. You'll gain valuable insight into your new career path, and if you're lucky, you might even get yourself a job offer out of it.

If your dream job involves working for yourself, networking is just as important. You need to build up the client base so you can afford to keep the light on. It's also helpful to build up a support system of other local entrepreneurs, so that you have a network of people who you can bounce ideas off of, or ask for help when you're stuck.

Opportunity Comes in Many Forms; Not Just Jobs

Don't get stuck finding a job, or starting a business for that matter. There are lots of opportunities in between that can enable you to turn your passion into your work. I like to call this range the Complete Opportunity Spectrum. Sure, you can get a job doing X, but what about a project, a consulting opportunity, an internship, licensing a business, becoming a franchisee, partnering up with an organization, or doing some temp work. Break away from the "get a job" mentality. There are lots of ways to make money doing just about anything...if you're creative enough.

Find Others with Shared Values

Passion is driven by emotion, but a raw hunger to learn, pursue, explore, and engage exist in a special kind of euphoric state. And if you haven't experienced it yourself, you really should. That's the key to loving what you do. Others love the same things you love, too, and value the same things, ideals, and principles. Go find them. Online, offline, it doesn't matter. Spend as much time as you can in these circles to fire you up and learn. So much starts to happen when you discover your sweet spot.

Hatch a Plan

Like any major life change, switching to a career you're passionate about takes some good, old-fashioned planning.

If your dream job involves working for yourself, you need a business plan, and a saving plan, so your career change doesn't spell financial disaster. Consider this you exit strategy, and take the time to crunch some numbers. How much income will you need to net, after taxes, insurance, and business expenses, to make ends meet, and how are you going to meet those goals? Most entrepreneurs don't turn a profit right away, so it's a good idea to save up a least a year's worth of expenses. Even if you don't end up having to tap into that nest egg, you'll be glad you have it in case of an emergency.

Looking to work for your dream employer? Read up on the company, and familiarize yourself with the industry. Do you need additional training to get the job you want? Take some classes, or look for an internship where you can learn the skills you need to get that ideal job. If there isn't a particular opening or position that you have you eye on, stalk the company's Web site for job listings. It may feel like applying through a company Web site sends your resume into a black hole, but that isn't always the case.

Conclusion

Thank you again for choosing this book!

I hope this book was able to help you to get started on ways to move into a new career change.

Once you have your passion clearly identified, you really should created your own map of that universe. All the industries, companies, organizations, experts, educational resources, websites, etc., that are significant in any way to that one thing, should be mapped out.

Finally, if you enjoyed this book, would you be kind enough to leave a review for this book on Amazon? It'd be greatly appreciated!

Thank you and good luck!

Check Out My Other Books

Below you'll find some of my other popular books that are popular on Amazon and Kindle as well. Alternatively, you can visit my author page on Amazon to see other work done by me.

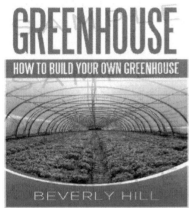GREENHOUSE: HOW TO BUILD YOUR OWN GREENHOUSE.

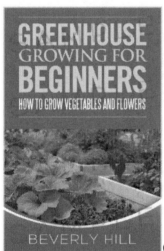GREENHOUSE GROWING FOR BIGINNERS: How to grow Vegetables and Flowers.

FREE BOOK
Beginners Guide to Yoga & Meditation

"Stressed out? Do You Feel Like The World Is Crashing Down Around You? Want To Take A Vacation That Will Relax Your Mind, Body And Spirit? Well this Easy To Read Step By Step

E-Book Makes It All Possible!"

Instructions on how to join our mailing list, and receive a free copy of "Yoga and Meditation" can be found in any of my Kindle eBooks.

NOTES

NOTES

NOTES

NOTES

NOTES

46205558R00019

Made in the USA
Middletown, DE
26 July 2017